CATCH A Wave

WHAT are WAVES?

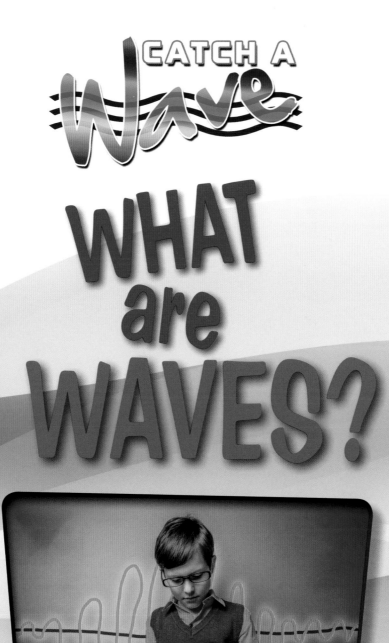

Heather C. Hudak

Crabtree Publishing Company
www.crabtreebooks.com

Crabtree Publishing Company

www.crabtreebooks.com

Author: Heather Hudak

Series research and development: Reagan Miller

Editorial director: Kathy Middleton

Editor: Janine Deschenes

Proofreaders: Ellen Rodger, Petrice Custance

Design: Ken Wright

Cover design: Ken Wright

Photo research: Heather Hudak, Ken Wright

**Production coordinator and
   Prepress technician:** Ken Wright

Print coordinator: Margaret Amy Salter

Animation and digital resources produced for
Crabtree Publishing by Plug-In Media

Library and Archives Canada Cataloguing in Publication

Hudak, Heather C., 1975-, author
        What are waves? / Heather Hudak.

Includes index.
(Catch a wave)
Issued in print and electronic formats.
ISBN 978-0-7787-2964-8 (hardcover).--
ISBN 978-0-7787-2972-3 (softcover).--
ISBN 978-1-4271-1858-5 (HTML)

        1. Waves--Juvenile literature. 2. Wave-motion, Theory of--
Juvenile literature. 3. Wave mechanics--Juvenile literature.
I. Title.

QC157.H83 2017   j531'.1133   C2016-907058-1
                                                                     C2016-907059-X

Library of Congress Cataloging-in-Publication Data

Names: Hudak, Heather C., 1975- author.
Title: What are waves? / Heather Hudak.
Description: New York, New York : Crabtree Publishing Company, [2017] |
    Series: Catch a wave | Includes index.
Identifiers: LCCN 2016059053 (print) | LCCN 2016059911 (ebook) |
    ISBN 9780778729648 (reinforced library binding) |
    ISBN 9780778729723 (pbk.) |
    ISBN 9781427118585 (Electronic HTML)
Subjects: LCSH: Wave mechanics--Juvenile literature. | Electromagnetic
    waves--Juvenile literature. | Wave-motion, Theory of--Juvenile literature.
Classification: LCC QC174.2 .H83 2017 (print) | LCC QC174.2 (ebook) |
    DDC 530.12/4--dc23
LC record available at https://lccn.loc.gov/2016059053

Crabtree Publishing Company

www.crabtreebooks.com   1-800-387-7650

Printed in Canada/032017/BF20170111

Published in Canada
Crabtree Publishing
616 Welland Ave.
St. Catharines, Ontario
L2M 5V6

Published in the United States
Crabtree Publishing
PMB 59051
350 Fifth Avenue, 59th Floor
New York, New York 10118

Published in the United Kingdom
Crabtree Publishing
Maritime House
Basin Road North, Hove
BN41 1WR

Published in Australia
Crabtree Publishing
3 Charles Street
Coburg North
VIC, 3058

CONTENTS

Hi, I'm Ava and this is Finn. Welcome to the world of waves! In this book you will discover the properties and patterns of waves.

After reading this book, join us online at Crabtree Plus to learn more about wave patterns, types, and uses! Just use the Digital Code on page 23 in this book.

WHAT ARE WAVES?

Have you ever seen a flag flapping at the top of a pole? You can watch as the wind makes waves across the fabric. Maybe you have seen waves on a body of water, such as a lake. Boats rise and fall as they bob over the waves. These are just a few kinds of waves. Did you know there are also many other types of waves that you cannot see? Some waves make the sounds we hear and the colors we see.

Waves in water are often created by wind. They are a type of wave that we can see.

Waves are Everywhere

Whether or not you can see them, waves are all around us. In fact, they are part of almost everything we do. We use waves to talk to people. Waves bring us the sights and sounds we see on television or hear on the radio. Some waves even help us cook food or send text messages. These are just a few kinds of waves. Light waves are rays, or beams of **energy**, that you can see with your eyes. Sound waves are made when an object **vibrates**. They carry sounds to our ears. Other waves we can feel. They create heat or cause the ground to shake.

A wave is a **disturbance** that happens over and over again in a regular pattern. A disturbance is an action that interrupts something from its **rest position**. For example, wind can cause water to move up and down from its still position. The wave carries the energy from the wind from one point to another as it moves.

ENERGY IN WAVES

Energy is the power needed to do work. We need it to cook food or light a room. We even need it to go for a walk or ride a bike.

There are many different forms of energy. Once energy is made, it does not disappear. It just changes from one form to another. Imagine you are riding a bike. You use a form of energy in your body to pedal. As you move your legs, the energy from your body **transfers** to the bike to get it moving. The energy takes on a different form. In this way, energy passes from one object to another. Energy moves from one place to another in waves.

Feel the Force

To create a wave, a **force** is needed to create a disturbance. Force is the push or pull on an object that happens when it interacts with another object. Applying a force to an object can make the object move, change direction, or change shape. Waves are created by a force.

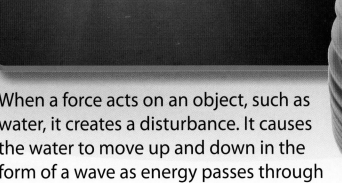

WHAT DO YOU THINK?

Stretch out a slinky from one end to the other. Take one end in your hand and shake it. What happens? How does the motion of the slinky relate to waves, energy, and force?

When a force acts on an object, such as water, it creates a disturbance. It causes the water to move up and down in the form of a wave as energy passes through it. When the force stops, the energy moving through the water stops, too. As the energy runs out, the waves in the water stop moving.

WAVE MOTION AND PATTERNS

When a ball flies through the air or a car speeds down a highway, it is in **motion**. Motion is what happens when something moves to a new place or position. All waves are in motion.

Waves move in a regular **pattern**. A pattern is something that happens over and over again. A wave has a repeating pattern of highs and lows. There are two basic types of wave motion: transverse and longitudinal.

Transverse Waves

Have you ever seen people do the wave at a sports game? One person stands up just as the next person sits down, and the wave goes around the stadium. This is an example of a transverse wave. The high point of a transverse wave is called a **crest**. The low point of a wave is called a **trough**.

Crest

Trough

Longitudinal Waves

Imagine standing side by side with a few of your friends. What would happen if you lightly bumped the person next to you with your shoulder? That person would wobble into the next person and so on. This is similar to the way a longitudinal wave moves.

Longitudinal waves move horizontally, or back and forth. Sometimes the waves are close together. This is called **compression**. Compression is similar to the crest of a transverse wave. Other times, the waves are spread out. This is called **rarefaction**. It is similar to the trough of a transverse wave.

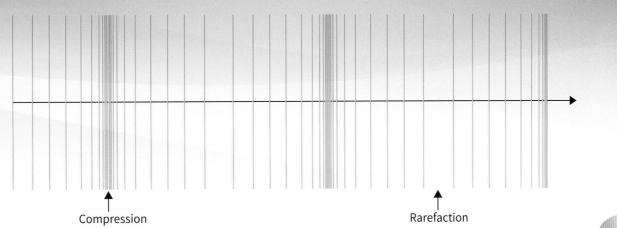

Compression

Rarefaction

WAVES IN WATER

Have you ever tried skipping rocks on a lake? When the rock hits the water, it makes a wave. The wave pushes against the water to make another wave and so on. You can see the waves ripple outward in a circle from the place where the rock landed. After a while, the waves lose their energy, and the water stills.

A wave in water is a disturbance in a **medium**. A medium is the substance or material that carries energy. In the example above, the medium is the water, and the rock causes the disturbance. The rock being skipped across the water is a force that creates energy. The waves carry or **transmit** energy away from the disturbance.

Wind, Water, and Waves

Wind causes most of the waves we see in bodies of water such as oceans and lakes. The wind causes a disturbance in the water as it blows across the surface. The waves move in the same direction the wind blows.

Wind is the movement of air. It is a force of energy. When it comes in contact with water, energy travels from the air to the water. This creates a wave. Similar to the rock example, one wave pushes against another to make even more waves.

Waves cause the water to move up and down as the energy passes through it. The water itself does not move forward. It is only the energy that moves with the waves. When the water stills, it simply drops in the same place it was before the wind started blowing.

Wind

Crest

Trough

WHAT DO WAVES HAVE IN COMMON?

All waves move in a similar motion, with regular patterns of highs and lows. Think about the waves in water. Each one has a crest and a trough.

All waves share the same basic **properties**. Properties are qualities that things have, such as size, speed, and power. The properties of waves include **amplitude**, **wavelength**, and **frequency**. We can use these properties to observe and measure wave patterns. Take a look at this diagram showing each of the common properties of waves.

Amplitude

Amplitude

The amplitude is the height of a wave from its rest position to the crest or the trough.

Trough

Frequency

These properties can help us identify similarities and differences in wave patterns. Even though all waves have the same properties, waves of the same type can differ in these properties. This is how we hear different sounds or see different colors.

Wavelength

The wavelength is the distance from one point on a wave to the same point on the next wave. It is often measured from crest to crest or trough to trough.

Wavelength

Crest

Frequency

The frequency refers to how often wave crests or troughs happen in a certain period of time.

WHAT IS AMPLITUDE ?

How do we know how tall a wave is? We can tell the height of a wave from its amplitude. It is the maximum distance of the wave from the rest position of the medium. It can be measured from either the crest or the trough.

Amplitude can be constant or it can **vary**. It all depends on the type of medium as well as other factors, such as the amount of energy that it carries. Imagine you are throwing a small pebble into the water. The pebble does not have a lot of force, so the waves it makes will be small, or have low amplitude. Now imagine you are jumping into a puddle. The force of you jumping will be much bigger than the pebble's force, so the waves you make will be quite high, or have high amplitude.

Tall or Short?

The more energy a wave has, the higher its amplitude will be. This means a wave with a high amplitude will be tall, and a wave with a low amplitude will be short. A wave with a high amplitude has high energy, while a wave with a low amplitude has low energy. If a light wave has low amplitude, it produces a dim light. By contrast, a high-energy light creates a bright light. It has high amplitude.

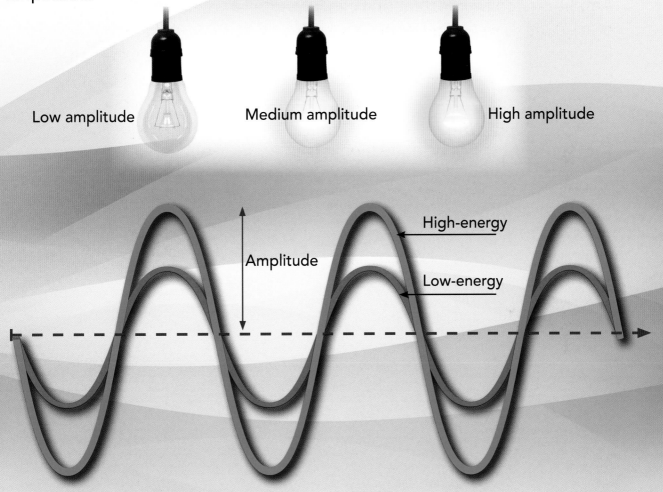

Low amplitude   Medium amplitude   High amplitude

Amplitude

High-energy

Low-energy

This chart shows the amplitude of a high-energy sound wave and a low-energy sound wave. A sound wave with higher energy has a higher amplitude. It would sound louder than a sound wave with a lower energy and amplitude. A wailing siren on a fire truck is a sound with high amplitude. It is very loud and can be heard from far away. When you whisper to your friend at school, you are making a sound with low amplitude.

WHAT IS WAVELENGTH?

How can you tell how long a wave is? Wavelength is the measure of the distance from one point on a wave to the same point on the next wave. Wavelength is the length of one cycle of a wave.

In a transverse wave, wavelength is most often measured from crest to crest or trough to trough. In a longitudinal wave, it is measured from one compression or rarefaction to the next. But on either type of wave, it can be measured from any two equal places on back-to-back waves.

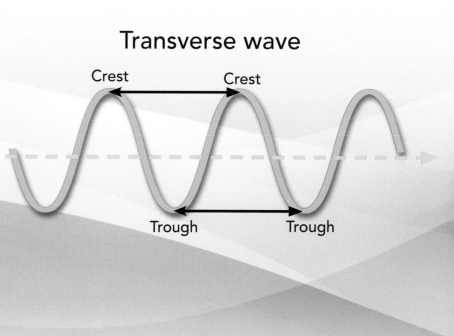

Transverse wave

Crest   Crest

Trough   Trough

Longitudinal wave

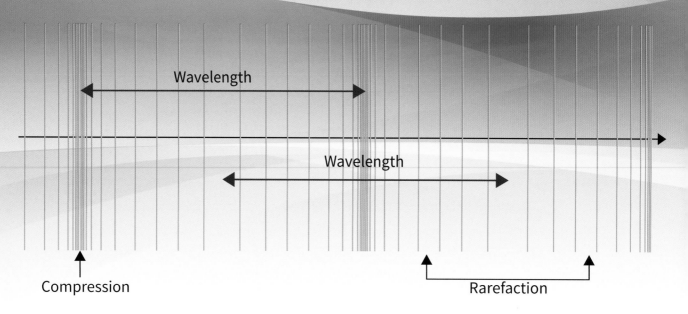

Wavelength

Wavelength

Compression

Rarefaction

Long or Short

Wavelengths can be long or short. The size of the wavelength changes the way we hear, see, or feel waves. In sound waves, longer wavelengths have a lower, or deeper, **pitch**. If a sound wave has a shorter wavelength, it will have a higher pitch. The colors you see also depend on the wavelength of a light wave. If the wavelength changes, so does the color you see. Warmer colors, such as red and orange, have longer wavelengths than cooler colors, such as blue and purple.

Shorter wavelength

Longer wavelength

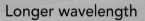

Imagine you are floating in the ocean. You can see the top of one wave, and in the distance, you see the top of the next wave. The distance from the top of one wave to the next is the wavelength.

WHAT IS FREQUENCY?

How often do waves occur? Frequency refers to the number of waves that pass through a fixed point in a specific period of time. Most often, wave frequency is measured in seconds. We usually measure frequency by determining how many waves happen, or pass by, per second.

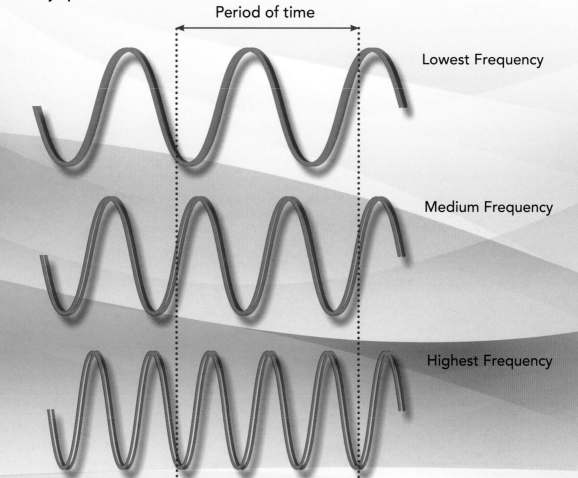

Period of time

Lowest Frequency

Medium Frequency

Highest Frequency

Take a look at the three different waves shown here. The top wave has the fewest crests and troughs in the period of time. It has the lowest frequency. The middle wave has a higher frequency. It has more crests and troughs in the same period of time. The bottom wave has many more crests and troughs than the top and middle waves. It has the highest frequency of the three waves.

Highs and Lows

Waves can have either high or low frequency. A high-frequency wave has more waves per second than a low-frequency wave. Both amplitude and frequency affect the energy of a wave. A wave with a higher frequency has more energy. This means it also has higher amplitude. Waves with a high frequency have a shorter wavelength. This means they have more crests and troughs per second. Waves with a low frequency have a longer wavelength. This means they have fewer crests and troughs per second.

In sound waves, frequency affects the pitch of the sound. A wave that has a high frequency has a short wavelength. There are many waves very close together. The sound it makes will be high pitched, such as an ambulance siren or a dolphin squeal. A wave with a low frequency has a longer wavelength. The waves will be spread wider apart. The sound it makes will have a lower pitch, such as a dog's growl or a cow's moo.

The tuba is a brass instrument. It makes sound waves from the vibrations of a player's lips. A tuba is a very large instrument, so the sound waves have a long way to travel through its brass tubes. Since waves lose energy as they travel, the tuba's large size means that its sound waves have a low frequency—and a very low pitch.

THE FORCE OF WAVES

Did you know that waves have another thing in common? All waves transfer energy. In other words, waves move energy from one place to another.

Fill a large bowl with water. Dip your finger in the water. Your finger is a force that makes a disturbance. It creates a wave that carries energy through the water. One wave leads to another wave as energy passes from one to the next.

Notice how the waves move away from your finger toward the edge of the bowl. They move one after the other, but they do not bunch together at the edge of the bowl. This is because the water itself does not move forward with the wave. Energy transfers from one wave to the next, moving from one place to another as it goes. But the medium the wave travels through does not go anywhere. Energy moves through the water without the water moving to a new place.

WHAT DO YOU THINK?

Wind is a source of energy that you can feel around you. Imagine the force of wind is applied to water. What happens to the wind energy?

If you don't move your finger or take it out of the water, the water eventually returns to its rest position. This is because the force is no longer being applied. But if you move your finger in and out of the water, you create more waves. As long as you keep pulling your finger in and out of the water, the force of your movement creates a disturbance in the water—which makes waves. As long as a wave has a source of energy, it can travel unchanged over long distances.

WAVES IN MOTION

When waves move through water, they move energy from one place to another. The water can move up and down, or side to side, but it does not travel to a new place. When the energy has passed through the water, the waves stop, and the water returns to its rest position.

Imagine a rubber duck is placed in a bathtub filled with water. If you made waves in the water, the duck would bob up and down with the waves. But the duck does not move across the water. When the waves stop moving and the water returns to its rest position, the duck will still be in the same place. This is because waves do not move the medium itself. The waves only transfer energy through the medium.

*If a **buoy** moves on the water, it is not because of the waves. It is because of other forces, such as wind.*

Have you ever seen a buoy on the ocean? It moves up and down as waves transfer energy from one place to another. But the buoy is in the same place when the waves stop moving and the water returns to its rest position. This is because the medium, or water, does not move with the waves.

Sound in Motion

Sound waves are another type of energy that relies on a force. When you pluck a string on a guitar, the force causes the string to vibrate. The vibrating string transfers energy into the air in the form of sound waves. Pianos and drums work the same way. When you tap a key on a piano or hit a drum with a stick, the force causes the objects to vibrate.

WHAT DO YOU THINK?

Try tying a rope to a tree. Place a ring in the center of the rope. Then gently wave the free end of the rope up and down. Be careful to keep the rope level, so that one side is not angled toward the ground. What do you think will happen to the ring? Record your results. Now try it again, but hold the free end of the rope lower than the end tied to the tree. Will the ring move now? Why or why not?

CHANGING WAVES

Have you ever tried to play a wind instrument, such as a **flute**? Wind instruments create sound waves when you blow into them. The force of the air makes vibrations that carry sound to your ears. The harder a person blows, the more force they are applying. This increases the amplitude of the sound waves. When playing an instrument such as a flute, the effect of the increase in amplitude is an increase in the volume of the sound.

The more amplitude a wave has, the more energy it has. This means the more force there is causing the disturbance, the higher the amplitude will be. Higher amplitude waves carry a higher amount of energy. Sound waves with higher amplitude are louder, just as light waves with a higher amplitude are brighter. When sound and light waves have lower amplitude, they are quieter and dimmer.

Higher or Lower, Longer or Shorter

Amplitude is just one property that affects the amount of energy a wave carries. Frequency is also important. When the amplitude is higher, it means more waves will pass through a point in a certain period of time. This means the wave has a higher frequency. In sound waves, this means it will have a higher pitch. Waves with a lower frequency have a lower pitch.

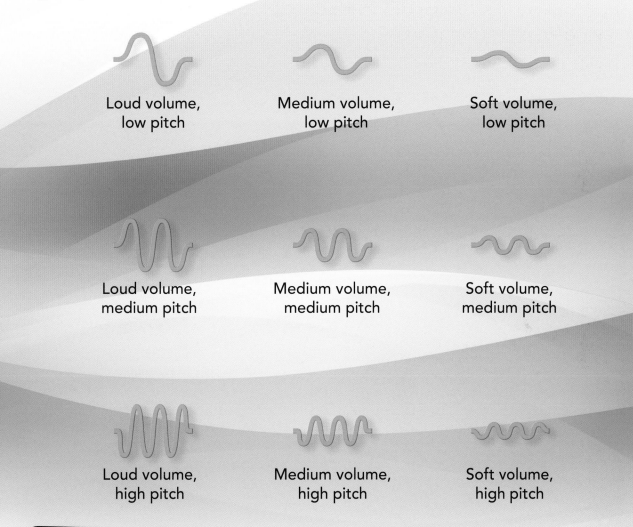

Loud volume,
low pitch

Medium volume,
low pitch

Soft volume,
low pitch

Loud volume,
medium pitch

Medium volume,
medium pitch

Soft volume,
medium pitch

Loud volume,
high pitch

Medium volume,
high pitch

Soft volume,
high pitch

When frequency changes so does wavelength. If the frequency is higher, the wavelength gets shorter. By contrast, longer wavelengths have shorter frequencies. The colors we see are determined by the wavelength. Violet has the shortest wavelength, while red has the longest wavelength.

MAKING WAVES

When it comes to waves on the water, their height depends on how long and strong the wind blows. A gentle wind makes ripples or small waves. The stronger the wind blows, the bigger the waves get. They form **peaks** that the wind grabs onto and pushes even higher. As waves increase in amplitude, they also increase in frequency. If a strong wind blows for a long time, very large, destructive waves can form.

Breaking Waves

As waves carry energy, they continue to move through the water. Some waves travel thousands of miles before they hit land. As waves near the shoreline, they begin to slow down and get taller. Eventually, the wave hits the shoreline. When this happens, the wave crest topples over and breaks, releasing its energy.

Waves and Coastlines

As waves crash against the **coastline**, they push sand upward. The sand washes back into the ocean as the water recedes. Depending on the wind direction, waves can hit the coastline at an angle. They also push sand and other **sediment** up the shoreline at an angle. In this way, the waves shape the coastline. They move rocks, sand, and other sediment sideways along the coastline.

WHERE DO WAVES COME FROM?

Many people think waves come from the water. They actually come from a force acting on the water. The force transfers energy to the water, making waves. Energy moves through each wave, causing the waves to move up and down. But the water stays where it is. You can observe this by making your own waves in a pan filled with water.

Experiment

How do waves move energy?

Materials

1 dishpan that is at least 4 inches (10 cm) deep
1 paper fan
1 electric fan
1 jug of water to fill the pan
1 toy boat

Procedure

1. Fill the pan about halfway with water. Place the boat in the water.
2. Stand approximately 12 inches (30 cm) from the pan, and use the paper fan to make waves on the water.
3. Observe what happens to the waves and the water. Do the waves get closer together or splash over the top at the far end of the pan? Does the boat move across the water with the waves?
4. Next, repeat the experiment with the electric fan on a low speed set approximately 12 inches (30 cm) from the pan.
5. What happens to the waves and the boat?

Share Your Results

In the first experiment, you used a paper fan and an electric fan to make waves on the water. In your notebook, write down which fan made waves with a higher amplitude. Explain why. Which waves had higher frequency? Which had longer wavelength? Record your results.

Next, share your findings with a friend who has done the same experiments. How were your results similar? How were they different? Explain why. Be sure to include words such as energy, force, and wavelength in your responses.

What Happened and Why?

As wind blows across water, it creates waves. The stronger wind from the electric fan made bigger waves than the paper fan. They had more energy and bigger amplitude. This also meant they had a higher frequency and shorter wavelength than the paper fan. The boat bobbed up and down on the waves, but it did not move in the direction of the waves. This is because waves move energy from one wave to the next. They do not move the water itself.

Learning More

Light, Sound, and Waves Science Fair Projects (Physics Science Projects Using the Scientific Method) by Robert Gardner. Enslow Publishers, 2010.

Ocean, Tidal, and Wave Energy: Power from the Sea by Lynn Peppas. Crabtree Publishing Company, 2008.

Science of Color: Investigating Light (Science in Action) by Karen Latchana Kenney. Checkerboard, 2016.

Websites

GCSE Bitesize: General Properties of Waves
Learn more about waves and their common features.
http://bbc.in/1fgSB4V

One Geology Kids: Waves
Learn more about ocean waves and their effect on coastlines.
www.onegeology.org/extra/kids/earthprocesses/waves.html

For fun wave challenges, activities, and more, enter the code at the Crabtree Plus website below.

www.crabtreeplus.com/waves

Your code is:
caw17

Glossary

Some **boldfaced** words are defined where they appear in the text.

buoy An anchored float
coastline A line that forms the boundary between land and ocean
compression The act of squeezing or pressing something together
disturbance An action that interrupts an object from its rest position
energy The power to do work
flute A type of wind instrument made from a long tube with holes in it
medium Something that is used to carry or transmit something else, such as a signal
peak Highest point of an object

pitch A high or low sound
rarefaction A reduction in the density of an object or the closeness of waves
rest position The place where a wave would sit if it had no energy
sediment Matter that settles at the bottom of something
transfer Move from one place to another
transmit To send a signal
vary To make differences between items
vibrate To cause something to move back and forth quickly

Index